Near Cornbury Park

Footnotes on a Landscape – 4

OXFORDSHIRE PLACE-NAMES

A CONCISE DICTIONARY

DAVID WHITTAKER

wavestone
press

For Penny and Alice – a celebration of our
twentieth year in Oxfordshire

OXFORDSHIRE PLACE-NAMES: A CONCISE DICTIONARY

ISBN: 0-9545194-4-2

WAVESTONE PRESS
6 ROCHESTER PLACE, CHARLBURY, OXON OX7 3SF, UK
Tel: 01608-811435
Email: wavestone@btinternet.com
Web: www.wavestonepress.co.uk

Acknowledgements:
This dictionary owes its existence to the pioneering work of many previous scholars. In
particular Eilert Ekwall, A. H. Smith and Margaret Gelling. I am humbly indebted to the
English Place-Name Society at the University of Nottingham for providing such
outstanding volumes of learned knowledge (see Further Reading).

Any errors in the text are down to this plebeian author's inadequate application by
way of research.

With gratitude to the anonymous illustrator of the map used in this book. At the time
of going to press all attempts to locate them for permission of use were unsuccessful.

Front endpaper: Dragon Hill.
Rear endpaper: Troy Town maze.

The series *Footnotes on a Landscape* is a personal engagement, by David Whittaker,
with the *genius loci* or 'spirit of place' of certain localities via artists, writers,
place-names, folklore, history, archaeology, topography etc.

Thanks to Keith Rigley for stylish layout and informed input.

Printed by Information Press, Eynsham, Oxon.

CONTENTS

MAP OF OXFORDSHIRE

Finmere A421

A41 (Akeman Street)

Piddington

Mixbury
Newton Purcell
Stratton Audley
Ambrosden
Lower Arncott
Upper Arncott

Juniper Hill
Cottisford
Shalswell
Hetha
Fringford
Coversfield
Launton
Alchester (Roman Town)

A43
Souldern
Tusmore House
Hardwick
Stoke Lyne
Bucknall
Bicester
Wendlebury
Weston-on-the-Green
Marton
Shipton-on-Cherwell

Clifton
Fritwell
Somerton
Ardley
Middleton Stoney
Chesterton

A41
Adderbury
Barford St. Michael
Barford St. John
Upper Hayford
Lower Hayford
Caulcott
Kirtlington
Wendlebury

Claydon
Clattercote A361
R. Cherwell
Wardington
Mollington
Cropredy
Gt. Bourton
Hanwell
Castle
Drayton
Abbey
Banbury
Oxford Canal
Bodicote
Milton
Bloxham
Deddington
Hampton
Nether Worton
N. Aston
Duns Tew
Middle Aston
Steeple Aston
Rousham House
Tackley
Kirtlington Park
Blatchingdon

Horton
Horley
Alkerton
Balscote
Wroxton
Shutford
Shenington
Epwell
Swalcliffe
Sibford Gower
Sibford Ferris
Hook Norton
Milcombe
Wigginton
Swerford
Over Norton
S. Newington
S. Newington
Over Worton
Gt. Tew
Lit. Tew
Ledwell
Sandford St. Martin
Westcot Barton
Middle Barton
Steeple Barton
Radford
Kiddington Hall
Glympton House
Wootton

A423
A422
Gt. Rollright
Roll right Stones
Lit. Rollright
Over Norton
Heythrop
Heythrop House
Gagingwell
Lidstone
Enstone
Spelsbury
Ditchley Park
Stonesfield
Woodstock
Cornbury Park

A34
Chastleton House
Salford
Cornwell
Chipping Norton
Churchill
Chadington
Sarsden Lodge
Ascott-under-Wychwood
Shorthampton
Chilson
Charlbury
Fawler

A436
Kingham
A424
Idbury
Fifield
Milton-under-Wychwood
Shipton-under-Wychwood
Bruern Abbey
Eyenlode
Wychwood Forest

6

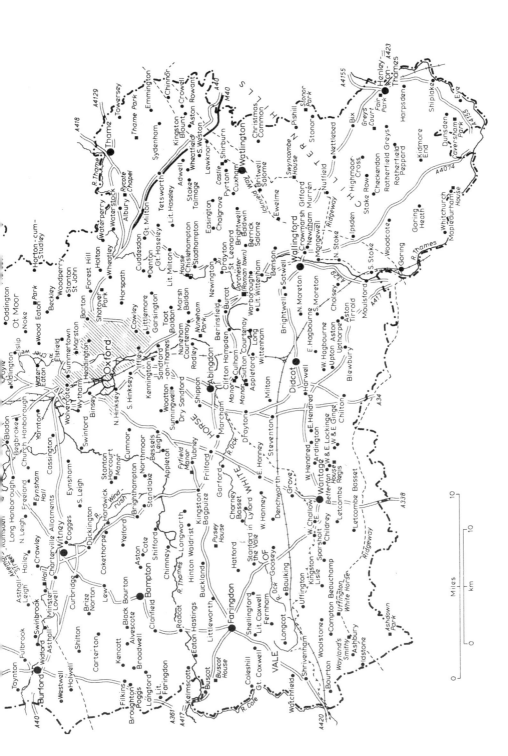

INTRODUCTION

WHAT'S IN A NAME?

As we speed around the countryside or sit in traffic jams, cocooned in our tin cans, we take the names on road signs and maps very much for granted. We live with them all our lives, they've become a part of our daily vocabulary and we rarely relate them to the surrounding environment; but that is where they have their roots. It's easy to overlook the fact that they can be a rich source of social and natural history, archaeology and topography. They are a kind of linguistic fossil helping to articulate the changes that have occurred in the landscape for well over a thousand years.

A serious study of place-names requires some widely informed detective work and there are many pitfalls for the unwary toponymist (from the Greek *topos* 'place' and *onoma* 'name'). It is important to remember that place-names were spoken long before they were written down. They were in a sense an oral map for, amongst other things, guiding people across an often hostile terrain between settlements, indicating the ease of access or otherwise across various topographical features, particularly rivers and floodplains; they also located springs, forests, tracks, clearings, ploughland, pastures, marshland, flora and fauna and could even give clues to the weather in a region. Gradually they got transcribed for a variety of reasons including estate and land survey-ing, ecclesiastical records, tithes, deeds, charters, taxes and as maps became more widespread. Spellings were phonetic and probably didn't take into account dialectical variations. This is especially true of that monumental chronicle the Domesday Book (1086), when names were collected by Norman-French civil servants who would have found the accents and dialects of local people very foreign indeed. The problem is compounded by spellings becoming further corrupted over the centuries. Therefore beware: what seems an obvious meaning from the spelling of a place can prove to be something quite different.

Philologists, dealing with the structure and development of language, have painstakingly pieced together likely meanings for most place-names; nevertheless puzzles remain and, erring on the side of caution, the words 'probably' and 'possibly' recur throughout this text. Research by the English Place-Name Society and intrepid individuals is ongoing and the academic debate over meanings can sometimes be very contentious. A concise dictionary such as this cannot provide the scope to discuss what are often highly technical issues, much bigger books already exist and can be found listed in Further Reading. Gelling (1984 and 2000) and Cameron (1996) give a particularly good overview of the problems.

NAMES WITHIN NAMES

Many place-names refer to a personal, tribal or family name. In most cases little or nothing is known about the Anglo-Saxon celebrities and their tribes who were deemed worthy of having tracts of land named after them (Hook Norton, Wychwood and Sunningwell are examples of the latter).

Much later with the Norman conquest came the feudal families whose names became affixed to the place where they held their manor (e.g., Britwell Salome, Compton Beauchamp, Nuneham Courtenay). Certain individuals also lent their names to a place or a feature in their possession (e.g., Carterton) while others put in an appearance as part of folklore and legend (e.g., Taston, Wayland Smithy, Grimsbury).

THE FORMAT OF THIS BOOK

All of the towns, villages and notable features of the county have been included except for farm names and field names. Here is a simple example:

WOODSTOCK
Wudestoce ca. 1000; Wodestoch DB. Woodland settlement [wudu, stoc].

The place-name in bold is followed, in italics, by the earliest recorded spelling with date, if known, and the Domesday Book (DB) spelling, if there is one. The most likely definition follows. Finally the place-name elements are included in square brackets. In a few instances several spellings have been supplied. Here is a slightly more complex case:

ROTHERFIELD GREYS/PEPPARD
Redrefeld DB; Rotherfeld Grey 1313; Ruderefeld Pippard 1255. Open land where cattle graze. Affixes from de Grey and Pipard families [hryther, feld].

Here we follow the same rules as Woodstock but with the addition (affix) of the French lords of the manor who acquired this land after the Norman conquest.

For the sake of concision certain places, such as Little Tew, Great Tew and Duns Tew are listed thus: **TEW, LITTLE/GREAT/DUNS**; similarly with North Aston, Middle Aston and Steeple Aston; but not with Hook Norton and Brize Norton as these are quite distinct places (not that everywhere isn't a distinct place in its way, and I accept, with apologies, that this is not always a consistent method of grouping).

ABBREVIATIONS

c.   century
ca.   circa
DB   Domesday Book 1086
EPNS   English Place-Name Society
ME   Middle English
OE   Old English
OF   Old French
p.n.   personal name
r.n.   river name
t.n.   tribe name

GLOSSARY

Glossary of place-name elements in the text; all Old English unless otherwise stated (the letters þ and ð, called *thorn* and *eth* respectively, have been modernised as *th*):

āc oak-tree
æppel apple
æsc ash-tree
ald old
amore bunting
assa ass
bæth bath, bathing place
bār boar
bēam trunk of tree carved for building
beorg hill or mound
beorht bright, clear
beorna warrior
bere birch-tree
blæc black, dark coloured
blēo variegated soil
bōcland land granted by charter
bold a building
bōt wood where useful timber is found
brād broad
brōc brook
brycg bridge
Bryt Briton
bucca he-goat
bulla bull
burh stronghold, fortification
burna spring or stream
byxe box-tree
cærse water-cress
cald cold
ceacce lump applied to a hill
cealc chalk
cealf calf

cearre   a turn or bend
ceastel   heap
ceaster   fort
ceorl   freeman or peasant
cēping   market-place
cild   child
cirice   church
cisel   gravel, shingle
clæg   clayey soil
clæne   clean
clif   cliff or bank
cogge   cog wheel
col   coal or charcoal
colt   colt
corn   crane
cot   cottage
cran   heron or crane
crāwe   crow
cumb   hollow or valley
cyning   king
denu   valley
dīc   ditch
dræg   slipway, portage or dray
dūn   hill
ēa   river, stream
east   east
ēg   island
ende   end of an estate or district
fāg   variegated or multi-coloured
fearn   fern
fēawe   few
feld   open country
fenn   fen or marsh
fif   five
fina   wood-pecker
flōr   floor or pavement
ford   ford or shallow place for crossing a stream
forst   ridge-like hill
fox   fox
freht   divination (as in 'wishing-well')
fūl   foul or filthy
gægan   to turn aside

gærsen   growing with grass

gama   games or sport

gāra   triangular plot of land

gōs   goose

geat   opening or gap

gelād   difficult river crossing

gīfete   plover

gold   gold

græf   pit

grāf   grove

grēne   green

grīma   mask

hæsel   hazel

hæth   heath

halh   nook or corner of land

halig   holy or sacred

hām   homestead, manor, estate

hamm   enclosure or water-meadow

hana   cock

hār   grey

hēafod   headland

hēah   high

healh   nook

hēg   hay

hengest   horse or stallion

henn   water-hen

hens   flock of hens

heorde   herd

hīd   a hide of land (ca. 120 acres)

hīwan   household

hlæw   burial mound

hlāw   mound or hill

hlyde   noisy stream

holh   hollow

horna   horn shaped

horning   bend or spit of land

hors   horse

horu   filth

hramsa   wild garlic

hrēod   reed or rush

hrycg   ridge, narrow hill

hryther   ox

huntena   hunters
hwæte   wheat
hwīt   white
hyll   hill
hymele   hop plant
hyrst   hillock
hyth   port or haven
īg   island
-ing   place characterised by, place belonging to
-ing-   associated with, called after
-inga-   possessive case of -ingas
-ingas   people of, followers of
lāc   play, sport
lache   slow stream
lacu   stream or watercourse
land   land
landriht   land rights
lang   long
lēah   woodland clearing
līn   flax
lytel   little
mære   boundary
mapuldor   maple-tree
mere   pool
merece   wild celery
mersc   marshland
middel   middle
mixen   dung-hill
mōr   moor
mynster   monastery
netel   nettle
nīwe   new
north   north
ōfer   slope, hill
ōra   border or margin
other   other, second
pæth   path or track
peose   pea
pīl   arrow, shaft, spike, pile
pirige   pear-tree
pise   pease
pohhede   baggy

port haven, harbour
portmann townsman, burgess
postel doorpost or gatepost
rād riding on horseback
rēad red
rīth stream
rithig small stream
ryge rye
sænget clearing
salt salt
sand sand
sceācere robber
scēad separation or boundary
sceald shallow
scēap sheep
scēne bright, beautiful
scēot steep slope
scīr bright, shining
scrifen decree, allot, pass sentence
scylf shelf
scypen cow-shed
sīd spacious, extensive
slæd valley, dell
slæp slippery muddy place
stān stone
stīepel steeple
stoc secondary settlement
stoccing clearing of stumps
stōd a stud or herd of horses
stow holy place or place of assembly
stræt street
styfic stump
sulh plough
sumor summer
swealwe swallow
swēora neck of land
swīn swine or pig
tacca young sheep
tāde toad
thorn thorn-tree
throp hamlet, outlying farm
thūma dwarf

tiēwe   row or ridge
tōh   tough
trēo   tree
tūn   farmstead, estate, village
twī   double, two
upp   up, higher up
wæter   watery place
walh   serf, foreigner, Briton
wanian   fluctuating stream
weald   woodland
weard   watch, ward, protection
weg   way, path, road
wella/welle   well, spring or stream
west   west
wīc   dairy farm
wierpels   path
wiht   bend
wīthig   willow-tree
worth   enclosure
wrocc   buzzard
wudu   woodland
yppe   raised place or platform

Woodstock Carnival

DICTIONARY

ABINGDON
abbandune 968; Abbendone DB. Æbbaor's or Æbbe's hill [p.n., dūn].

ADDERBURY
Eadburggebyrig ca. 950; Edburgberie DB. Ēadburh's stronghold [p.n., burh].

ADWELL
Adwelle DB. Eadda's spring or well [p.n., wella].

AKEMAN STREET
Accemannestrete 12thc. Roman road from Bath to St Albans, uncertain first element [stræt].

ALBURY
Aldeberie DB. Ealda's or old stronghold [p.n. or ald, burh].

ALCHESTER
Alencestre ca. 1160. Relates to a Roman fort (the first element may be the Romano-British place-name *Alauna*) [ceaster].

ALKERTON
Alcrintone DB. Ealhhere's farmstead [p.n., tūn].

ALVESCOT
Elfegescote DB. Ælfhēah's cottage(s) [p.n., cot].

AMBROSDEN
ambresdone DB. Ambre's hill or hill of the bunting [p.n. or amer, dūn].

ANDERSEY ISLAND
Andresia ca. 1104. Andrew's island so named from the Church of St Andrew [ēg].

APPLEFORD
Æppelford ca. 895; Apleford DB. Ford where apple-trees grow [æppel, ford].

APPLETON
Æppeltune 942; Apletune DB. Farmstead where apples grow [æppel, tūn].

ARDINGTON
Ardintone DB. Possibly 'farmstead associated with Earda' [p.n., -ing-, tūn].

ARDLEY
eardulfes lea 995. Eardwulf's clearing [p.n., lēah].

ARNCOTT, UPPER/LOWER
Earningcote 983; Ernicote DB. Cottage(s) associated with a man named Earn [p.n., -ing-, cot].

ASCOTT-UNDER-WYCHWOOD
Estcot 1220. Eastern cottage(s) near Wychwood forest [ēast, cot].

ASHBURY
Eissesberie DB. Stronghold where ash-trees grow [æsc, burh].

ASSENDON, MIDDLE/LOWER
Assundene 10th c. Assa's valley or valley of the ass [p.n. or assa, denu].

ASTERLEIGH
Exle 1185. Eastern clearing [ēast, lēah].

ASTHALL
Esthale DB. East nook of land [east, halh].

ASTON, NORTH/MIDDLE/STEEPLE
estone DB; Stipelestun 1220. East farmstead. Later prefix refers to church steeple [stīepel, ēast, tūn].

ASTON ROWANT/TIRRALD
Estone DB; Aston Roaud 1318; Aston Torald. Affix R. from Rowald de Eston 13th c.; T. from the Thorald family 12th c. [ēast, tūn].

ASTON UPTHORPE
Eastune 964; Estone DB; Aston et Upthrop 1316. Higher east farmstead, in relation to A. T. [east, tūn, upp, throp].

ATTINGTON
Attendune DB. Eatta's hill [p.n., dūn].

BABLOCK HYTHE
Babbelack 1277; Bablick Hithe 1797. Babba's stream; later addition OE hyth 'landing place' [p.n., lacu].

BADGEMORE
Begevrde DB. Probably 'Bæcga's ridge' [p.n., hrycg].

BAINTON
badintone DB. Bada's farm [p.n., -ing, tūn].

BALDON, MARSH/TOOT
baldedone DB; Mersse Baldindon 1241; Totbaldindon 1316. Bealda's hill. M. prefix from Richard de la Mare 13th c.; T. from ME *tote* 'look-out hill' [p.n., dūn].

BALSCOTE
Berescote DB. Bælli's cottage(s) [p.n., cot].

BAMPTON
Bemtun 1069; Bentone DB. Probably 'farmstead made of beams' [bēam, tūn].

BANBURY
Banesberie DB. Banna's stronghold [p.n., burh].

BARFORD ST JOHN/ST MICHAEL
Bereford DB. Barley ford. Affix from local churches [bere, ford].

BARNARD GATE
Barnard Yate 1725. Probably 'Bernard's gate' [p.n., geat].

BARTON, MIDDLE/STEEPLE/SESSWELL'S/WESTCOTE
Bertone DB; Mydell Barton 1449; Stepelbertone 1247; Barton Sharshill 1517; Westcote Berton 1242. Barley farmstead. St. from church steeple; Se. refers to William de Shareshull 14th c.; W. is west cottage(s) [middel, west, cot, stīepel, bere, tūn].

BAULKING (BALKING)
Bedalacinge ca. 870. Uncertain, probably 'pool' referring to a tributary of the River Ock [bæth].

BAYNARD'S GREEN
Bayard's Green 1724. Bayard is the name of a bay horse. Tournaments were held here from at least the 12th c.

BAYWORTH
Began wyrthe 956. Bæga's enclosure [p.n., worth].

BECKLEY
Beccalege 1005; Bechelie DB. Becca's woodland clearing [p.n., lēah].

BEGBROKE
Bechebroc DB. Becca's brook [p.n., brōc].

BENSON
Bænesington c. 900; Besintone DB. Farmstead associated with Benesa [p.n., -ing-, tūn].

BERRICK SALOME
Berewiche DB; Berwick Sullame 1571. Barley farm. Affix from the family of Almaric de Suleham 13th c. [bere-wīc].

BESSELS LEIGH
Leie DB; Besilles Lee 1538. Woodland clearing. Prefix from the family name of Petrus Besyles 15th c. [lēah].

BETTERTON
Bedretone DB. Probably 'Bethere's farmstead' [p.n., -ing-, tūn].

BICESTER
Bernecestre DB. Beorna's or warrior's fort [p.n. or beorna, ceaster].

BINFIELD HEATH
Benifeld 1177. Beona's field or open land where bent grass grows [p.n. or beonet, feld].

BINSEY
Beneseye 1122. Byni's island [p.n., ēg].

BIX
Bixa DB. Box-tree wood [byxe].

BLACK BOURTON
Burtone DB. Fortified farmstead. Prefix possibly refers to the black habits of the monks of Osney, Austin Canons, who had land here ('black habits' in the sense of garments, not in the sense of dark compulsive behaviour) [burh, tūn].

BLACKTHORN
Blaketorn 1190. Blackthorn [blæc-thorn].

BLADON
Blade DB. From a Celtic river-name of uncertain origin (old name of the Evenlode).

BLENHEIM
The palatial residence earned by the Duke of Marlborough's victory in Blenheim, Bavaria, 1704.

BLETCHINGDON
Bleccesdone DB. Blecci's hill [p.n., dūn].

BLEWBURY
Bleobyrig 944; Blidberia DB. Hill-fort with variegated soil [blēo, burh].

BLOXHAM
Bloxham DB. Blocc's homestead [p.n., hām].

BOARS HILL
Boreshulla 1170. Hill of the boar [bār, hyll].

BODICOTE
Bodicote DB. Boda's cottage(s) [p.n., -ing-, cot].

BOLNEY COURT
Bollehede DB. Probably 'landing place for bullocks' [bulena, hyth].

BOTLEY
Boteleam 12th c. Bōta's woodland clearing or where timber is acquired [p.n. or bōt, lēah].

BOULD
Bolda 13th c. Building [bold].

BOURTON, LITTLE/GREAT
Burton 1209. Fortified farmstead [burh, tūn].

BRIGHTHAMPTON
Byrhtelmingtun 984: Bristelmestone DB. Beorhthelm's farmstead [p.n., tūn].

BRIGHTWELL BALDWIN
Berhtanwellan 887; Britewelle DB. Bright or clear spring. Affix from Sir Baldwin de Bereford 14th c. [beorht, wella].

BRIGHTWELL
Beorhtawille 854; Bricsteuuelle DB. As above.

BRITWELL SALOME
Britwelle DB; Brutewell Solham 1320. Possibly 'spring of the Britons'. Affix from the de Sulham family 13th c. [Bryt, wella].

BRIZE NORTON
Nortone DB; Northone Brun 13th c.; Brunesnorton 1341. North farmstead. Prefix from William le Brun 1200 [north, tūn].

BROADWELL
Bradewelle DB. Broad stream [brad, welle].

BROOKHAMPTON
Hantone DB; Brochampton DB. Probably 'farm homestead by a brook' [hām, tūn, brōc].

BROUGHTON
Brahtone DB. Farmstead by a brook [brōc, tūn].

BROUGHTON POGGS
Brotone DB; Broughton Pouges 1526. Farmstead by a brook. Affix from Sir Robert Pugeys [brōc, tūn].

BRUERN
Bruaria 1159. Possibly OF *bruiere* meaning 'heath'.

BUCKLAND
Boclande 957; Bocheland DB. Land granted by charter [bōcland].

BUCKNELL
Buchehelle DB. Bucca's hill or where bucks graze [p.n. or bucca, hyll].

BULLINGDON
Bulesden 1179. Bulla's or bulls' valley [p.n. or bulla, denu].

BURCOT
Bridicote 1198. Bryda's cottage(s) [p,n., cot].

BURDROP
Burithorp 1314. Hamlet by the fortification [burh, throp].

BURFORD
Beorgeford 752; Bureford DB. Stronghold by a ford [burh, ford].

BUSCOT
Boroardescote DB. Burgweard's cottage(s) or cottage(s) of the fort-keeper [p.n. or burh-weard, cot].

CADWELL COVERT
Cadewelle DB. Cada's spring or stream [p.n., wella].

CANE END
Canonende 16th c. Refers to the canons at the monastery of Notley.

CARSWELL MARSH
Chersvelle DB; Carsewell Merssh 1467. Spring or stream where cress grows. Later addition ME *mershe* 'marsh' [cærse, wella].

Charlbury with Wychwood Forest

CARTERTON

William Carter purchased this land from the Duke of Marlborough in 1901 to create a smallholders' colony.

CASSINGTON

Cersetone DB. Farmstead where cress grows [cærse, tūn].

CASWELL

Cauereswell 1166; Cressewell 1182. Cāfhere's well or cress-stream well [p.n. or cærse, wella].

CAULCOTT

Caldecot 1199. Cold cottages [cald, cot].

CAVERSFIELD

Cavrafelle DB. Cāfhere's open land [p.n., feld].

CHADLINGTON

Cedelintone DB. Farmstead associated with Ceadela [p.n., -ing-, tūn].

CHALFORD

Chalcford 1185. Chalk ford [cealc, ford].

CHALGROVE

Celgrave DB. Chalk pit [cealc, græf].

CHALLOW, EAST/WEST

Ceawanhlǣwe 947; Ceveslane DB. Ceawa's tumulus [p.n., hlāw].

CHARLBURY

Ceorlingburh ca. 1000; Cherleberiam 1109: Churlebiry 1197; Charlebury 1320; Chorlebury 1428; Chorlbury 1429. Stronghold associated with Ceorl [p.n., -ing-, burh].

CHARLTON

Ceorlatun 956; Cerletone DB. Farmstead of the freemen [ceorl, tūn].

CHARLTON-ON-OTMOOR

Cerlentone DB; Cherleton upon Ottemour 1314. Farmstead of the freemen near Otmoor [ceorl, tūn].

CHARNEY BASSETT

Ceornei 821; Cernei DB. Probably 'island on the River Cern'. The latter from Welsh *carn* 'rocks, stones'. Affix from the Basses family [ēg].

CHARTERVILLE ALLOTMENTS

Named from the Chartist movement 1847.

St Peter's, Charney Bassett

CHASTLETON
Ceastelton 777; Cestitone DB. Farmstead by a prehistoric camp [ceastel, tūn].

CHAWLEY
Chaluel 1241. Pasture for calves [cealf, lēah].

CHECKENDON
Cecadene DB. Ceacca's valley or valley by the hill [p.n. or ceacce, denu].

CHESTERTON
Cestertune 1005; Cestretone DB. Farmstead by a Roman fort [ceaster, tūn].

CHILDREY
Cillarthe 950; Celrea DB. Cilla's or Cille's stream [p.n., rīth].

CHILSON
Cildestuna ca. 1200. Young man's farmstead [cild, tūn].

CHILSWELL
Chiefleswelle ca. 1180. Cifel's stream [p.n., wella].

CHILTON
Cylda tun ca. 895. Young man's farmstead [cild, tūn].

CHIMNEY
Ceommanyg 1069. Ceomma's island in a marsh [p.n., ēg].

CHINNOR

Chennore DB. Ceonna's slope [p.n., ōra].

CHIPPING NORTON & OVER NORTON

Nortone DB; Chepingnorthona 1224; Caldenorton 1217; Spitulnortun 1217; Overenorton 1302. North farmstead with a market. O.N. previously 'cold north farmstead' overlooking Ch.N. The priory of Cold Norton was founded by Avelina, daughter of Ernulf de Hesding lord of the manor of Norton 1086; a hospital was built here slightly later: ME *spital* [cēping, north, tūn].

CHIPPINGHURST

Cibbaherste DB. Cibba's wooded hill [p.n., hyrst]

CHISELHAMPTON

Hentone DB; Chiselentona 1147. High gravely farmstead [cisel, hēah, tūn].

CHOLSEY

Ceolesig ca. 895; Celsei DB. Cēol's island in the marsh [p.n., ēg].

CHRISTMAS COMMON

Christmas Coppice 1617. Place where holly-trees were abundant.

CHURCHILL

Cercelle DB. Hill with or near a church [cirice, hyll].

CLANFIELD

Chenefelde DB. Clean field [clæne, feld].

Bliss Mill, Chipping Norton

CLARE
Claiora ca. 1130. Clay slope [clæg, ōra].

CLATTERCOTE
Clatercota 1167. Possibly 'cottage(s) by a clatter' from the dialect word *clatter* meaning 'loose stones or debris' [cot].

CLAYDON
Cleindona 1109. Clay hill [clæg, dūn].

CLEEVE
Cleeve 1788. Cliff or slope [clif].

CLEVELEY
Clivelai 1194. Slope clearing [clif, lēah].

CLIFTON
Cliftona ca. 1170. Farmstead on or near a slope [clif, tūn].

CLIFTON HAMPDEN
Cliftona 1146. Farmstead on or near a slope. Affix from 1836 the Hampden family [clif, tūn].

COGGES
Coges DB. Cog-shaped hills [cogg].

COLESHILL
Colleshylle 10th. c.; Coleselle DB. Probably 'Coll's hill' [p.n., hyll].

COMBE
Cumbe DB. Valley [cumb].

COMPTON BEAUCHAMP
Cumtune 955; Contone DB; Cumton Beucamp 1236. Valley farmstead. Affix from the de Beauchamp family 13th c.

COOKLEY GREEN
Cokelea ca. 1183. Cuca's clearing [p.n., lēah].

CORNBURY PARK
Corneberie DB. Stronghold frequented by cranes or herons [corn, burh].

CORNWELL
Cornewelle DB. Stream frequented by cranes or herons [corn, wella].

COTE
la Cote 1203. Cottage(s) [cot].

COTHILL
Cothill 1783. Cottage(s) on a hill [cot, hyll].

COTTISFORD
Cotesforde DB. Cott's ford [p.n., ford].

COWLEY
Couelea 1004; Couelie DB. Cufa's clearing [p.n., lēah].

COXWELL, LITTLE/GREAT
Cocheswelle DB. Probably 'Cocc's stream or well' [p.n., wella].

CRAWLEY
Croule 1214. Woodland clearing frequented by crows [crāwe, lēah].

CROPREDY
Cropelie DB. Probably 'Croppa's small stream' [p.n., rithig].

CROWELL
Clawelle DB. Crow's spring or well [crāwe, welle].

CROWMARSH GIFFORD
Cravmares Gifford 1316; Cromershe Giffard 1316. Crow's marsh. Affix from Gifard 1086 [crāwe, mersc].

CUDDESDON
Cuthenesdune 956; Codesdone DB. Cūthen's hill [p.n., dūn].

CULHAM
Culanhom 821. Cūla's river meadow [p.n., hamm].

CUMNOR
Cumanoran 931; Comenore DB. Cuma's hill-slope [p.n., ōra].

CURBRIDGE
Crydan brigce 956. Creoda's bridge [p.n., brycg].

CUTSLOW
Cuthues hlaye 1004; Codeslave DB. Cūthen's burial mound [p.n., hlāw].

CUXHAM
Cuceshamm 955; Cuchesham DB. Cuc's river-meadow [p.n., hamm].

DEAN
Dene DB. Valley [denu].

DEDDINGTON
Dædintun 1050; Dadintone DB. Dæda's farmstead [p.n., -ing-, tūn].

DELLY END
Denle 1278. Valley clearing [denu, lēah].

DENCHWORTH
Deniceswurthe 947; Denchesworde DB. Denic's enclosure [p.n., worth].

DENTON
Denton 1122. Valley farmstead [denu, tūn].

DIDCOT
Dudecota 1206. Dudda's cottage(s) [p.n., cot].

DITCHLEY
Dicheleye 1208. Clearing by a ditch. Refers to Grim's Ditch (*Grimesdich 1300*). See Grimsbury [dīc, lēah].

DORCHESTER
Dorciccaestræ 731; Dorchecestre DB. Roman fort called Dorcii (uncertain Celtic name) [ceaster].

DRAGON HILL
Dragon Hill 1830. Situated just below the White Horse near Uffington. Reputed to be where St George slew the Dragon. The patch of bare chalk being where the blood issued from the fiendish wound poisoning the soil.

DRAYCOT
Draicote DB. Probably 'shed where drays or sledges are kept' [dræg, cot].

Didcot power station from the Ridgeway

DRAYTON

Draitone DB (near Banbury); *Draitune 958*; *Draitone DB* (near Didcot).
Farmstead by a portage or slope where drays are used [dræg, tūn].

DRAYTON ST LEONARD

Drætona 1146. As above with church dedication.

DRY SANDFORD

Sandforda 811; Sanford DB; Dry Sandford 18th c. Dry sandy ford [sand, ford].

DUCKLINGTON

Duclingtun 958; Dochelintone DB. Ducel's estate [p.n., -ing-, tūn].

DUNSDEN GREEN

Dunesdene DB; Donsden grene 1589. Dynne's valley [p.n., denu].

DUNTHORP

Dunetorp DB. Dunna's village or hill village [p.n., dūn, throp].

DUXFORD

Dudochesforde DB. Duduc's ford [p.n., ford].

EAST END

le Estend 1529 (North Leigh); *Estend 1316* (Chadlington); *East ende 1590*
(Hook Norton). [east, ende].

EASINGTON

Esidone DB. Ēsa's hill [p.n., dūn].

EATON

eatune 9th c.; Eltune DB. River farmstead [ēa, tūn].

EATON HASTINGS

Etone DB; Eton Hastinges 1298. As above. Affix from de Hastinges 12th c.

ELSFIELD

Esefelde DB. Elesa's open land [p.n., feld].

EMMINGTON

Amintone DB. Eama's farm [p.n., -ing-, tūn].

ENSTONE/CHURCH

Henestan DB; Churchenstane 1415. Enna's boundary stone [p.n., stān].

EPWELL

Eoppan wyllan 956. Eoppa's spring or stream [p.n., wella].

EWELME

Auuilme DB. River source [æ, welm].

EXLADE STREET

Hekeslad 1241. Possibly 'Ecgi's valley' [p.n., slæd].

EYNSHAM

Egenes homme 864; Eglesham DB. Possibly 'Ægen's river-meadow' [p.n., hamm].

FARINGDON

Færndunæ c. 971; Farendone DB. Fern covered hill [fearn, dūn].

FAWLER

Fauflor 1205 (near Stonesfield). Variegated floor (referring to the tessellated pavement of a Romano-British house) [fāg, flōr].

FAWLER

Flageflur ca. 1180 (near Kingston Lisle). Possibly 'flagstone floor' [flage, flōr].

FENCOT

Fencota 1146. Cottage(s) on marshy ground [fenn, cot].

FERNHAM

Fernham 9th c. River-meadow where ferns grow [fearn, hamm].

Fernham

FEWCOT

Feaucot 1185. Few cottages [fēawe, cot].

FIFIELD

Fifhide DB. Five hides of land [fif, hīd].

FILKINS

Filching 12th c. Possibly 'Filica's people' [p.n., -ingas-].

FINMERE

Finemere DB. Pool frequented by woodpeckers [fina, mere].

FINSTOCK

Finestochia 12th c. Outlying farmstead frequented by woodpeckers [fina, stoc].

FORDWELLS

Sewkeford 1300. (Originally Seofeca's ford.) Ford over a spring or stream [ford, wella].

FOREST HILL

Fostel DB. Hill with a ridge [forst, hyll].

FOSCOT

Foxcote DB. Probably 'foxes'earth' [fox, cot].

Near Finstock

FOXCOMBE HILL
foxhola cumbe 985. Valley of foxes' earth [fox, cumb].

FRILFORD
Frieliford DB. Frithela's ford [p.n., ford].

FRINGFORD
Feringeford DB. Probably 'Fēra's ford' [p.n., ford].

FRITWELL
Fertwelle Db. Possibly 'spring used for divination or wishing well' [freht, wella].

FULBROOK
Fulebroc DB. Foul or dirty brook [fūl, brōc].

FULWELL
Fulewell 13th c. Foul or dirty stream [fūl, wella].

FYFIELD
Fif Hidum 956; Fivehide DB. Five hides of land [fif, hīd].

GAGINGWELL
Gadelingwelle ca. 1173. Spring or well of the kinsmen or companions [gædeling, wella].

GANFIELD
Gamesfel, Gamenesfelle DB. Open land of games. A likely reference to a tournament linked to the holding of the hundred court [gama, feld].

GANGSDOWN HILL
Gangvlvesdene DB. Gangwulf's valley [p.n., denu].

GARFORD
Garanforda 940; Wareford DB. Gāra's ford or ford at triangular plot of ground [p.n. or gāra, ford].

GARSINGTON
Gersedun DB. Grassy hill [gærsen, dūn].

GINGE, EAST/WEST
Gainge 811; Gainz DB. From OE river name meaning 'one that turns aside' [gægan, -ing].

GLYMPTON
Glimtuna ca. 1050; Glintone DB. Farmstead on River Glyme (see Appendix 1) [r.n., tūn].

GODINGTON

Godendone DB. Gōda's hill [p.n., dūn].

GODSTOW

Godestowe ca. 1150. Place of God (from the Benedictine nunnery) [stow].

GOLDEN MANOR

Goldhora 987. Slope where golden flowers grow [gold, ōra].

GOOSEY

Goseie 9th c.; Gosei DB. Goose island [gōs, ēg].

GORING

Garinges DB. Settlement of Gāra's people [p.n., -ingas].

GOSFORD

Goseford 1242. Geese ford [gōs, ford].

GOZZARD'S FORD

Gozzard Field and Mead 1815. Probably a personal name.

GRAFTON

Graptone DB. Farmstead by a grove [grāf, tūn].

GREENFIELD

Grenefeld 1479. [grēne, feld].

All Saints, Goosey

GREYS GREEN

Greys Green 1840. From Walter de Grey.

GRIMSBURY

Grimberie DB. Stronghold of Grim. The name of some supernatural deity, possibly Woden (from OE *grīma* 'a mask', and refers to that god's inclination to appear in disguise) [grīma, burh].

GROVE

la Graue 1188. Grove [grāf].

HAGBOURNE, EAST/WEST

Haccaburna ca. 895; Hacheborne DB. Probably 'Hacca's stream' [p.n., burna].

HAILEY

Haylegh 1241. Clearing where hay is made [hēg, lēah].

HAMPTON GAY/POYLE

Hantone DB; Hamtona Gaitorum ca. 1130; Hampton Poile 1428. Home farm. Affixes G. from Reginald Gait 12th c.; P. from de la Puile family 13th c. [hām, tūn].

HANBOROUGH, CHURCH/LONG

Haneberge DB. Hagena's hill [p.n., beorg].

HANNEY, EAST/WEST

Hannige 956; Hannei DB. Island of wild birds [hana, ēg].

HANWELL

Hanewege DB. Hana's way [p.n., weg].

HARDWICK

Hardewich DB (near Bicester); *Herdewic 1199* (near Witney). Herd farm [heorde, wīc].

HARPSDEN

Harpendene DB. Probably 'valley of the harp' (from the shape) [denu].

HARWELL

Haranwythe 956; Harvvelle DB. Spring or stream by a hill called Hāra (the grey one) [hār, wella].

HASELEY, LITTLE/GREAT

Hæseleia 1002; Haselie DB. Hazelwood clearing [hæsel, lēah].

HATFORD

Hatford DB. Headland ford [hēafod, ford].

HEADINGTON
Hedenandun 1004; Hedintone DB. Hedena's hill [p.n., dūn].

HEATH END
Heath End 1797. Probably from William de la Hethe ca. 1219.

HEMPTON
Henton DB. High farm [hēah, tūn].

HEMPTON WAINHILL
Winehelle DB. Possibly 'Willa's corner'; H. from nearby Henton [p.n., halh].

HENDRED, EAST/WEST
Hennarith 956; Henret DB. Stream frequented by wild birds [henn, rīth].

HENLEY-ON-THAMES
Henleiam ca. 1140. High clearing [hēah, lēah].

HENSINGTON
Hansitone DB. Possibly 'hens' farmstead' [hens, tūn].

HENTON
Hentone DB. High farmstead [hēah, tūn].

HEN WOOD
Hynewode 12th c. Wood of the monastic community [hīwan, wudu].

HETHE
Hedha DB. Heath [hæth].

HEYFORD, UPPER/LOWER
Hegford DB. Ford used during hay-making [hēg, ford].

HEYTHROP
Edrope DB. High hamlet or outlying farmstead [hēah, throp].

HINKSEY
Hengestesige 10th c. Hengest's island or island of the stallion [p.n., hengest, ēg].

HINTON WALDRIST
Hentone DB; Henton Walrushe 1591. High farmstead. Affix from de Sancto Walerico 12th c. [hēah, tūn].

HOLCOMBE, LITTLE/GREAT
Holecumba 1154. Hollow valley [holh, cumb].

HOLTON
Healhtunes 956; Eltone DB. Farmstead in nook or corner of land [healh, tūn].

HOLWELL
Holewella 1189. Holy spring or stream [halig, wella].

HOOK NORTON
Hocneratune 10th c. Possibly 'farmstead of the Hoccanēre tribe' [t.n., tūn].

HORLEY
Hornelie DB. Clearing in horn-shaped land [horna, lēah].

HORMER
Hornemeres ca. 1050; Hornimere DB. Pool of the dwellers in the horn of land [horna, -inga, mere].

HORNTON
Hornigeton 1194. Farmstead by the horn-shaped land [horning, tūn].

HORSPATH
Horspadan DB. Horse path [hors, pæth].

HORTON-CUM-STUDLEY
Hortun 1005; Stodleya ca. 1180. H. is 'muddy farmstead'; S. is 'clearing for horses' [horu, tūn, stōd, lēah].

HUNTERCOMBE END
Huntercumba ca. 1183. Huntsmens' valley [huntena, cumb].

ICKNIELD WAY
Icenhylte 903. A continuation of Buckle Street (from Bourton-on-the-Water to Rotherham in Yorkshire). Meaning uncertain, possibly from the Iceni tribe.

IDBURY
Ideberie DB. Ida's stronghold [p.n., burh].

IDSTONE
Edwinestone 1199. Ēadwine's farmstead [p.n., tūn].

IFFLEY
Gifetelea 1004; Givetelei DB. Possibly 'woodland clearing of the plover' [gīfete, lēah].

IPSDEN
Yppesdene DB. Valley by an upland [yppe, denu].

ISLIP

Githslepe ca. 1050; Letelape DB. Slippery place by the River Giht (old name for River Ray) [r.n., slæp].

JUNIPER HILL

Jennaper Parocke ca. 1605. Uncertain meaning.

KELMSCOT

Kelmescote 1234. Cēnhelm's cottage(s) [p.n., cot].

KENCOT

Chenetone DB. Cēna's cottage(s) [p.n., cot].

KENNINGTON

Chenitun 821; DB. Cēna's farmstead [p.n., tūn].

KIDDINGTON

Chidintone DB. Cydda's estate [p.n., -ing-, tūn].

KIDLINGTON

Chedelintone DB. Cydela's farmstead [p.n., -ing-, tūn].

KIDMORE END

Kydmore end 16th c. Probably from a personal name.

KINGHAM

Caningeham DB. Homestead of Cæga's people [p.n., -inga-, hām].

KINGSTON BAGPUIZE

Cyngestun ca. 976; Chingestune DB; Kingeston Bagepuz 1284. King's estate or royal manor. Affix from Ralph de Bagpuize 11th c. [cyning, tūn].

KINGSTON BLOUNT

Chingestone DB; Kyngestone Blount 1379. As above. Affix from Hugo de Blund 13th c.

KINGSTONE LISLE

Kingeston 1220; Kyngeston Isle 1373. As above. Affix from del Isle family 13th c.

KINGSTONE WINSLOW

Kyngeston' Wendescleve 1252. As above. Affix means 'Wendel's cliff' [p.n., clif].

KIRTLINGTON

Kyrtlingtune ca. 1000; Certelintone DB. Cyrtla's farmstead [p.n., -ing-, tūn].

LANGFORD

Langefort DB. Long ford [lang, ford].

LANGLEY

Langeleiam 1199. Long clearing [lang, lēah].

LANGTREE

Langetrie ca. 1159. Tall tree [lang, trēo].

LASHBROOK

Lachebroc DB. Stream flowing through boggy land [lache, brōc].

LAUNTON

Langtune ca. 1050; Lantone DB. Long farmstead [lang, tūn].

LEAFIELD

La Felde 1213. Open land (with OF definite article) [feld].

LEDWELL

Ledewelle DB. Loud spring or stream [hlyde, wella].

LEIGH, NORTH/SOUTH

Lege DB; Nordelegh 1233; Suthleye 13th c. Clearing [lēah].

LETCOMBE BASSETT/REGIS

Ledecumbe DB; Ledecumbe Basset 1247; Ledecombe Regis 1344. Lēoda's valley. B. affix from Bassett family 12th c.; R. affix because it was owned by the Crown [p.n., cumb].

LEW

Hlæwe 984; Lewa DB. Mound or tumulus [hlæw].

LEWKNOR

Leofecanoran 990; Levecanole DB. Lēofeca's hill-slope [p.n., ōra].

LIDSTONE

Lidenestan 1235. Lēodwine's stone [p.n., stān].

LITTLEMORE

Luthlemoria ca. 1130. Little marsh [lytel, mōr].

LITTLEWORTH

Wyrthae ca. 971; Ordia DB. Little enclosure [lytel, worth].

LOCKINGE

Lacinge 868; Lachinges DB. The playful one (referring to the stream) [lāc, -ing].

LONGCOT
Cotes 1233; Longcote 1332. Long row of cottages [lang, cot].

LONGWORTH
Wurthe 958; Langewyrthe 1284. Long enclosure [lang, worth].

LYFORD
Linforda 944; Linford DB. Ford where flax grows [līn, ford].

LYNEHAM
Lineham DB. Enclosure where flax is grown [līn, hām or hamm].

MAIDENSGROVE
Menygrove 15th c. Probably 'common grove' [mære, grāf].

MAPLEDURHAM
Mapeldreham DB. Spring or stream where maples grow [mapuldor, hām].

MARCHAM
Merchamme 900; Merceham DB. River-meadow where celery grows [merece, hamm].

MARSTON
Mersttune ca. 1069. Farmstead by a marsh [mersc, tūn].

MERTON
Meretone DB. Farmstead by a pool [mere, tūn].

MIDDLETON STONEY
Mideltone DB. Probably 'middle farmstead with stony ground' [middel, tūn, stān].

MILCOMBE
Midelcumbe DB. Middle valley [middel, cumb].

MILTON
Middeltun 956; Middeltune DB. Middle farmstead [middel, tūn].

MILTON, LITTLE/GREAT
Mideltone DB. As above.

MILTON-UNDER-WYCHWOOD
Mideltone DB. Below Wychwood Forest.

MINSTER LOVELL
Minestre DB; Minestre Lovel 1279. Monastery or large church. Affix from the Luvel family 13th c. [mynster].

MIXBURY
Misseberie DB. Stronghold near a dunghill [mixen, burh].

MOLLINGTON
Mollintune ca. 1015; Mollitone DB. Moll's farmstead [p.n., -ing-, tūn].

MONGEWELL
Mundingwillæ ca. 970; Mongewel DB. Munda's stream [p.n., -ing-, wella].

MORETON, NORTH/SOUTH
Mortune 12th c. Moor farmstead [mōr, tūn].

MOULSFORD
Muleforda ca. 1110. Probably 'Mūl's ford' [p.n., ford].

MURCOTT
Morcot ca. 1191. Moorland cottage(s) [mōr, cot].

NEITHROP
Ethrop 1224. Hamlet (first element uncertain) [throp].

NETHERCOTE
Altera Cote DB. The other cottage(s) [other, cot].

NETTLEBED
Nettlebed 1246. Land overgrown with nettles [netele, bedd].

NEW YATT
Possibly new gate or opening [nīwe, geat].

NEWINGTON
Niwantun ca. 1045; Nevtone DB. New farmstead [nīwe, tūn].

NEWNHAM MURREN
Niwanham 966; Neuueham DB; Neweham Mungewell 1268. New homestead or manor. Affix from Richard Morin 13th c. [nīwe, hām].

NEWTON PURCELL
Niveton 1198; Newentone Purcel 1285. As above. Affix from the Purcell family 1198.

NOKE
Acam DB. Oak-tree [āc].

NORTHBROOK
Norbroc, Northbrok DB. [brōc].

41

NORTHMOOR

More 1059; Northmore 1367. North marsh [north, mōr].

NUFFIELD

Tocfeld ca. 1180. Probably 'tough open land' [tōh, feld].

NUNEHAM COURTENAY

Nenham DB; Newenham Courteneye 1320. New homestead. Affix from Curtenay family 13th c. [nīwe, hām].

OAKLEY

Hakeley 1215. Oak-wood [āc, lēah].

ODDINGTON

Otendone DB. Otta's hill [p.n., dūn].

OSNEY

Osanig 1004. Ōsa's island [p.n., ēg].

OTMOOR

Ottanmere 1005. Otta's marsh [p.n., mersc].

OXFORD

Oxnaforda ca. 925; Oxeneford DB. Ford used by oxen [oxa, ford].

PIDDINGTON

Petintone DB. Pyda's farmstead [p.n., -ing-, tūn].

PILING HILL

Pyle 1476. Shaft [pīl].

PISHILL

Pesehull 1195. Hill where peas grow [peose, hyll].

PLAY HATCH

Playhatch 1603. Probably village sports related.

PLOUGHLEY

Pokedelawa 1169. Probably 'baggy barrow or tumulus' referring to its shape [pohhede, hlāw].

POFFLEY END

Pouwele 13th c. Probably 'Pohha's stream' [p.n., wella].

PORT MEADOW

Portmanneheit ca. 1185. Burgher's islet [portmann, eyt].

PORT WAY

la Portweye 1210. Road leading to a town [port, weg].

POSTCOMBE

Postlecumbe 1246. Possibly 'valley gateway' [postel, cumb].

PUDLICOTE

Pudelicote 1176. Pudel's cottage(s) [p.n., cot].

PUSEY

Pesei DB. Island in marsh where peas grow [pise, ēg].

PYRTON

Piringtune 987; Peritone DB. Pear-tree farm [pirige, tūn].

RADCOT

Rathcota 1163. Reed or red cottage(s) [hrēod or rēad, cot].

RADFORD

Radeford DB. Probably 'ford which can be ridden across' [rād, ford].

RADLEY

Radelege ca. 1180. Red woodland clearing [rēad, lēah].

The Thames at Radcot

RAMSDEN
Rammesden 1246. Probably 'wild garlic valley' [hramsa, denu].

RIDGEWAY
hrycwæg 856. [hrycg, weg].

ROFFORD
Roppan forda 1002; Ropeford DB. Hroppa's ford [p.n., ford].

ROKE
Roke 1379. Oak [āc].

ROLLRIGHT, LITTLE/GREAT
Rollandri DB; Rollendricht 1091. Possibly 'an estate with special legal rights belonging to Hrolla'. The nearby Rollright Stones are a late Neolithic barrow with standing stones and stone circle (said to have been a king and his army petrified by a local witch) [p.n., landriht].

ROTHERFIELD GREYS/PEPPARD
Redrefeld DB; Rotherfeld Grey 1313; Ruderefeld Pippard 1255. Open land where cattle graze. Affixes from de Grey and Pipard families [hryther, feld].

ROUSHAM
Rowesham DB. Hrōtwulf's homestead [p.n., hām].

RYCOTE
Reicote DB. Cottage(s) where rye is grown [ryge, cot].

ST HELEN WITHOUT
The church of St Helen was in existence ca. 995 acording to records, and was probably founded a good deal earlier.

SALFORD
Saltford 777; Salford DB. Ford over which salt is transported [salt, ford].

SALT STREET/WAY
Saltstrete 1217. Route for transporting salt [salt, weg].

SANDFORD ST MARTIN
Sanford DB. Sandy ford. Dedication from church [sand, ford].

SANDFORD-ON-THAMES
Sandforda 1050; Sanford DB. As above.

SARSDEN
Secendene DB; Cerchesdena ca. 1180. Probably 'valley of the church' [cirice, denu].

The Rollright Stones

SATWELL
Sottewell ca. 1242. Probably a Berkshire family name.

SHELLINGFORD
Scaringaford 931; Serengeford DB. Ford of the people of Scear [t.n., -inga-, ford].

SHELSWELL
Scildeswelle DB. Scield's or shallow well [p.n. or sceald, wella].

SHENINGTON
Senendone DB. Beautiful hill [scēne, dūn].

SHIFFORD
Scipford 1005; Scipford DB. Sheep ford [scēap, ford].

SHILLINGFORD
Sillingeforda 1156. Probably 'ford of Sciela's people' [p.n., -inga-, ford].

SHILTON
Scylftune 1044. Farmstead on a ledge [scylf, tūn].

SHIPLAKE
Siplac 1163. Sheep stream [scēap, lacu].

All Saints, Shorthampton

SHIPPON

Sipene DB. Cattle-shed [scypen].

SHIPTON-ON-CHERWELL

Sceaptun 1005; Sciptone DB. Sheep farm by the River Cherwell [scēap, tūn].

SHIPTON-UNDER-WYCHWOOD

Sciptone DB. Sheep farm below Wychwood Forest.

SHIRBURN

Scireburne DB. Bright, clear stream [scīr, burna].

SHORTHAMPTON

Scorhamton 1227. Short farmstead [hām, tūn].

SHOTOVER

Scotorne DB. Steep slope [scēot, ōfer].

SHRIVENHAM

Scrifenanhamme ca. 950; Seriveham DB. River-meadow allotted to the church by decree [scrifen, hamm].

SHUTFORD

Schiteford ca. 1160. Probably 'Scytta's ford' [p.n., ford].

SIBFORD FERRIS/GOWER

Scipforde, Sibeford DB; Sibbard Ferreys 18th c.; Sibbeford Goyer 1220. Sibba's ford. Affixes from Robert de Ferrers (12th c.) and the Guher (13th c.) families [p.n., ford].

SIGNET

Senech 1285. Possibly 'place cleared by burning' [sænget].

SOMERTON

Sumertone DB. Summer farmstead [sumor, tūn].

SONNING COMMON

Sunnynge Commone 1606. (Place of) Sunna's people [t.n., -ing-].

SONNING EYE

Eye 1285; Sunning Eye 1761. Island near Sonning [ēg].

SOTWELL

Suttanwille 945; Sotwelle DB. Probably 'Sutta's well or stream' [p.n., wella].

SOULDERN

Sulethorne ca. 1160. Thorn-tree near a gully [sulh, thorn].

SOUTHROP

Suthrop 1316. South hamlet [south, throp].

SPARSHOLT

Speresholte 963; Spersolt DB. Woods where spear shafts are obtained or woods with spear traps [spere, holt].

SPELSBURY

Speolesbyrig ca. 11th c. Spēol's stronghold [p.n., burh].

STADHAMPTON

Stodeham ca. 1135. River-meadow where horses are kept [stōd, hamm].

STANDLAKE

Stanlache ca. 1155. Stony stream [stān, lacu].

STANFORD-IN-THE-VALE

Stanford DB; Stanford in le Vale 1496. Stony ford. Affix indicates proximity to the Vale of the White Horse [stān, ford].

STANTON HARCOURT

Stantone DB; Stantone Harecurt ca. 1275. Stone farmstead with possible reference to the nearby Devil's Quoits stone circle (removed to make way for a wartime runway). Affix from Robert de Harcourt 12th c. [stān, tūn].

STANTON ST JOHN

Stantone DB ; Stantona Johannis de Sancto Johanne 12th c. Farmstead on stony ground. Affix refers to church land and probable Knights Templars presence.

Near Spelsbury

Between Stonesfield and Fawler

STEVENTON

Stivetune DB. Farmstead associated with Stīf or farmstead by the tree-stump [p.n. or styfic, -ing-, tūn].

STOKE LYNE

Stoches DB. Outlying farmstead. Affix from a blending of the del Isle and Lynde families [stoc].

STOKE ROW

Stoke Rewe 1435. Probably 'row of houses on outlying farmstead'.

STOKE TALMAGE

Stoches DB; Stokes Talemasche 1219. Affix from Peter Thalemalche 12th c.

STOCKINGS, UPPER/LOWER

Stokkynges 1387. Place cleared of stumps [stoccing].

STONESFIELD

Stuntesfeld DB. Stunt's open land [p.n., feld].

STONOR

Stanora 10th c. Stony hill-slope [stān, ōra].

STOW WOOD

Stawode ca. 1142. Stony wood [stān, wudu].

STOWFORD
Stauuforde DB. Stony ford [stān, ford].

STRATTON AUDLEY
Stratone DB; Stratton Audeley 1318. Farmstead on a Roman road. Affix from the de Alditheleg family 13th c. [stræt, tūn].

SUGARSWELL
Shokerewellemore ca. 1260. Robbers' spring or stream by the fen [sceācere, welle, mōr].

SUGWORTH
Sogoorde DB. Sucga's enclosure [p.n., worth].

SUMMERTOWN
Summerstown 1822. Said to be named by a horsedealer James Lambourn, the first settler here, who called it Somers Town because of its pleasant position.

SUNNINGWELL
Sunnigwellan 9th c.; Soningennel DB. Spring or stream of the Sunningas tribe [t.n., -inga-, wella].

SUTTON
Sutton 1207. South farmstead [suth, tūn].

SUTTON COURTENAY
Suthtun ca. 870, Sudtone DB. As above. Affix from the Curtenai family 12th c.

SWALCLIFFE
Sualewclive ca. 1166. Slope frequented by swallows [swealwe, clif].

SWERFORD
Surford DB. Ford by a col [swēora, ford].

SWINBROOK
Svinbroc DB. Pig brook [swīn, brōc].

SWINFORD
Swynford 931. Pig ford [swīn, ford].

SWYNCOMBE
Svincumbe DB. Pig valley [swīn, cumb].

SYDENHAM
Sidreham DB. Broad enclosure [sīd, hamm].

TACKLEY
Tachelte DB. Tæcca's clearing or where young sheep are kept [p.n. or tacca, lēah].

TADMARTON, LOWER
Tademæton 956; Tademertone DB. Possibly 'farmstead by a frog pool' [tāde, mere, tūn].

TASTON
Thorstan 1278. Possibly 'Thor's stone' [p.n., stān].

TAYNTON
Tengetune ca. 1055. Possibly 'sprinkling (from Welsh *taen*) stream by a farmstead' [tūn].

TEMPLE COWLEY
Temple Couele ca. 1200. See Cowley. Land here was given to the Knights Templars in 1139.

TETSWORTH
Tetleswrthe ca. 1150. Tætel's enclosure [p.n., worth].

TEW, LITTLE/GREAT/DUNS
Tiwan 1004; Tewe, Teowe DB; Donestiua ca. 1210. Possibly 'ridge' or 'row'. Prefix from the name Dunn [tiēwe].

Great Tew

THAME
Tame ca. 1000; DB. Named from the River Thames.

THOMLEY
Tvmbeleia DB. Possibly 'woodland clearing haunted by dwarves' [thūma, lēah].

THRUPP
Trop DB. Outlying farmstead [throp].

TIDDINGTON
Titendone DB. Tytta's hill [p.n., dūn].

TOKERS GREEN
Talkers Green 1797. (Speaks for itself.)

TOWERSEY
Eie DB; Turrisey 1240. Island (of the de Turs family 13th c.).

TROY FARM
Troy House 1797. Takes its name from the turf maze cut in the grounds of a private house ca. 1600, also known as Troy Town. 'Troy' may be derived from the popular Roman game *Lusus Troiae* or Game of Troy. The word relates to 'turn' in various languages. Strictly speaking, this is a labyrinth rather than a maze. Labyrinths are unicursal, their convoluted paths always lead to the centre; mazes are multicursal, their paths may lead astray and include dead-ends.

TUBNEY
Tobenie DB. Tubba's island [p.n., ēg].

TUSMORE
Toresmere DB. Probably 'Thur's pool' [p.n., mere].

TYTHROP
Duchithorp DB. Double homestead [twī-, throp].

UFFINGTON
Uffentune 10th c.; Offentone DB. Uffa's farmstead [p.n., tūn].

UPTON
Upeton 1200. Upper farmstead [upp, tūn].

WALCOT
Walecote ca. 1130. Probably 'cottage(s) of the Britons' [walh, cot].

WALLINGFORD
Welengaford ca. 895: Walingeford DB. Ford of Wealh's people [p.n., -inga-, ford].

WANTAGE
Waneting ca. 880; DB. Fluctuating stream [wanian, -ing].

WARBOROUGH
Wardeberg 1200. Look-out hill [weard, beorg].

WARDINGTON, UPPER
Wardinton ca. 1180. Wearda's or Wærda's farmstead [p.n., tūn].

WARPSGROVE
Werplesgrave DB. Possibly 'grove pathway' [wierpels].

WATCHFIELD
Wæclesfeld 931; Wachenesfeld DB. Wæcel's or Wæccīn's open land [p.n., feld].

WATCOMBE
Watecvvmbe DB. Wheat valley [hwæte, cumb].

WATERPERRY
Perie DB; Waterperie ca. 1190. Watery place by the pear tree [wæter, pirige].

WATERSTOCK
Stock DB. Watery place [wæter, stoc].

Wayland Smithy

WATLINGTON

Wæclintune 887; Watelintone DB. Probably 'Wæcel's farmstead' [p.n., -ing-, tūn].

WAYLAND SMITHY

welandes smidthan 955. Wēland was the OE spelling of the smith of Germanic legend who married a Valkyrie. A stone age burial chamber (about 6000 years old). According to local lore a lame horse left here overnight, with some money, would be found the following day newly shod with fresh brogues. The proximity of the White Horse figure maintains the equine motif.

WEALD

Walda 1188. Woodland [weald].

WENDLEBURY

Wandesberie DB. Wændla's stronghold [p.n., burh].

WESTON-ON-THE-GREEN

Westone DB. West farmstead [west, tūn].

WESTWELL
Westwelle DB. Westerly spring or stream [west, wella].

WHEATFIELD
Witefelle DB. White open land [hwīt, feld].

WHEATLEY
Hwatelega 1163. Clearing where wheat grows [hwæte, lēah].

WHITCHURCH
Hwitecyrcan 990; Witecerce DB. White church [hwīt, cirice].

WHITE HORSE HILL
Whytehorse 1322. Named from the turf figure.

WIDFORD
Widiforde DB. Willow-tree ford [wīthig, ford].

WIGGINTON
Wigentone DB. Wicga's farmstead [p.n., tūn].

WILCOTE
Widelicote DB. Wifel's cottage(s) [p.n., -ing, cot].

WILLIAMSCOTT
Williamescote 1166. William's cottage(s) [p.n., cot].

WITNEY
Wyttanige 969; Witenie DB. Witta's island in a marsh [p.n., ēg].

WITTENHAM, LITTLE/LONG
Wittanham ca. 865; Witeham DB. Witta's river-bend [p.n., hamm].

WOLVERCOTE
Ulfgarcote DB. Wulfgār's cottage [p.n., -ing-, cot].

WOODCOTE
Wdecote 1109. Woodland cottages [wudu, cot].

WOODEATON
Eatone DB; Wudeetun 1185. Woodland farmstead by a river [wudu, ēa, tūn].

WOODSTOCK
Wudestoce ca. 1000; Wodestoch DB. Woodland settlement [wudu, stoc].

WOOLSTONE
Olvricestone DB. Wulfric's farmstead [p.n., tūn].

The River Glyme, Wootton (near Woodstock)

WOOTTON

Wuttune 985 (near Woodstock); *Uudetun 821* (near Abingdon). Woodland farmstead [wudu, tūn].

WORTON, NETHER/OVER

Ortune 1050; Hortone DB. Farmstead by a slope [ōra, tūn].

WRETCHWICK

Wrechewiche 1182. Possibly exile's dairy farm, from OE *wrecca*, an ancestor of modern wretch [wīc].

WROXTON

Werochestan DB. Probably 'buzzard's stone' [wrocc, stān].

WYCHWOOD

Huiccewudu 840. Forest of the Wicca tribe [t.n., wudu].

WYTHAM

Wihtham ca. 957; Winteham DB. Homestead in a river-bend [wiht, hām].

YARNTON

Ærdintune 1005; Hardintone DB. Earda's farmstead [p.n., -ing-, tūn].

YATSCOMBE

geatescumb 955. Probably 'valley of the gate' [geat, cumb].

YELFORD

Aieleforde DB. Ægel's ford [p.n., ford].

APPENDICES

APPENDIX 1

Selected River and Stream-Names

BAGMORE BROOK

baccan mor 931. Bacca's marsh [p.n., mōr].

BALDON BROOK

Humelibrok ca. 1240. Earlier name means 'where wild hop grows' [hymele, brōc].

BAYSWATER BROOK

Ludebroke ca. 1220; Bayard's Watering place 1676. Earlier name means 'loud brook'. 'Bayard' is the stock name for a bay horse.

CHERWELL

cearwellan 864. Probably 'winding stream' [cearre, wella].

CHILDREY BROOK

cille rith 940. See place-name.

CHILL BROOK

Lutteswelle 1261. Earlier spelling suggests *hlūtor* 'clear'. Later form means 'gully' [ceole].

COLDRON BROOK

Colthurne 1356. Possibly 'colt's corner' [colt, hyrne].

COLDWELL BROOK

Cawdell Brook 1591. Cold stream [cald, wella].

COLE

on lentan 931. Earlier spelling suggests Welsh *iliant* 'flood, stream'. For later form see Coleshill.

COLWELL BROOK

Coluullan broc 958. Charcoal stream (may relate to charcoal-burning in the area) [col, wella].

CUDDESDON BROOK

Cumbe Brok 1278. Rises in Coombe Wood [cumb].

CUTTLE BROOK

Cuttelehulle ca. 1270. Possibly 'intermittent stream' from German *kuötelbieke*.

DANES BROOK

Denebroke ca. 1294. Stream in a valley [denu].

DORN

A back formation from Dornford.

EVENLODE

Bladene 1005; Euenlode 1577. (Earlier form named from Bladon.) Eowla's crossing [p.n., gelād].

GALLOS BROOK

Gallesbrooke 1422. Brook by the gallows.

GINGE BROOK

Geenge 726. Maybe from OE *gægan* 'to turn aside'.

GLYME

Glim 958. Probably from Celtic *ghel* 'bright'.

The Evenlode Valley

HASELEY BROOK

Hazeley Brook 1822. See place-name.

HIGHFURLONG BROOK

Cranemeare 1551. Originally 'heron pool' [cran, mere].

ISIS

Isa ca. 1350. May come from the second part of *Tamesis* (see Thames). There may also be some lost association with the Egyptian goddess Isis.

LAND BROOK

land broc 947. Probably 'boundary brook' [land, brōc].

LETCOMBE BROOK

wanotingc broc 956. Fluctuating stream, as in Wantage.

LIMB BROOK

Buggan broc 1005. Earlier 'Bugga's stream'. The more recent name maybe a corruption of *Leigh ham Brook* 'river-meadow clearing'.

LOCKINGE BROOK

Lackincg 868. Possibly 'playful brook' [lāc].

MADLEY BROOK

Madelebroke 1298. May refer to a lost place called Madley.

MALLEWELL

Marwelle 1422. Boundary stream [mære].

MANUAL SPRING

mærwelle 956. Boundary spring [mære].

NOR BROOK

Northbroc 1252. North brook [north].

OCK

æoccænen 856. Possibly from the Celtic/British word *esāco* 'salmon'.

RAY

Geht 845. Maybe from the Welsh *iaith* 'language' meaning 'babbling brook'.

SARS BROOK

Sars Brook 1778. A back formation from Sarsden.

SHADWELL SPRING

Shadwell Field ca. 1840. Boundary [scēad].

SOR BROOK
Unknown.

STUTFIELD BROOK
Tealeburnan 959. Earlier form possibly from OE *getæl* 'quick, active'. Later form unknown.

SWERE
Swere 1577. A back formation from Swerford.

THAMES
Tamesis 51 BC (Caesar); Temese 940; Tæmese 966; Thamisia 1219. Possibly from a Celtic root *tam* 'dark' or pre-Celtic root *tā* 'melt, flow turbidly'.

TOMWELL
Thomewelle lake 1436. Possibly taken from Thomley.

TRILL MILL STREAM
Trillemyll ca. 1402. Origin uncertain.

WINDRUSH
weric, wenrices, wænric 958. Possibly a Celtic compound of Welsh *gwyn* 'white' and Irish *riasg* 'fen'.

APPENDIX 2
Selected Street-Names of Oxford

This small selection of streets has been chosen out of historic interest and curiosity value. The names of streets, unlike names of the landscape, do vary a great deal over the centuries, indicating changing fashions and activities.

BEAR LANE
Maybe *Schitebur' lan' ca. 1290; Shitebournelane 1358.* Early spellings give a flavour of the primitive plumbing facilities. Later named from the Bear Inn.

BEAUMONT STREET
Bello monte 13th c. Beautiful hill (a puzzle, as the area is flat).

BRASENOSE LANE
Vicus St Mildridae 13th c. After St Mildred's Church. Later name from the bronze sanctuary knocker of Brasenose Hall.

BREWER STREET

Sleyng Lane 1478; Sleyne Lane 1690; Brewers Streete early 17th c. Early spellings due to the number of butchers here, later became a residence of brewers.

BROAD STREET

Horsemongeres–streta ca. 1235; Broad Street 1750. Wide street built over the filled-in defense moat known as *Canditch*.

CARFAX

Carfox 1483; Quatervoys 1661. From the Latin *quadrifurcus* 'four-forked'.

CLARENDON STREET, LITTLE/GREAT

Named in the latter part of the 19th c. after the Clarendon Press (L.C. Street formerly Blackboy Lane).

CORNMARKET

Northyatestret 15th c. Named from a Cornmarket building erected in 1536 (and pulled down by soldiers in 1644 so the roof could be melted down into bullets).

FOLLY BRIDGE

Suthbriggestrete ca. 1225; South Bridge 1699. Called Folly Bridge since late 17th c. Refers to a tower on the bridge, now demolished, where Roger Bacon (ca. 1214-1295) pursued his astronomical studies. Known, in turn, as Batchelor's Tower, Friar Bacon's Study, New Gate and the Folly (as in ruinous building).

GEORGE STREET

Hyrismanstrete 1251; Irisshmanstrete 1407; Thames Street 17th c. Earliest spellings may relate to William de Hibernia, a local bailiff at the time. Later named after one of the Kings.

GLOUCESTER GREEN

Gloucester Greene, Glocester greene 1601. Named from Gloucester Hall, a Benedictine house connected to Gloucester Abbey (founded in 1283 and on the site of current Worcester College).

JERICHO

The city's first suburb, building commenced here in the 19th c. The name is taken from nearby Jericho Gardens first mentioned in 1688; a Jericho Inn also existed at this time. The name is indicative of remoteness.

LOGIC LANE

Horsemanlane 1247; Hormuln Lane 1661; Logick Lane 17th c.. There was once a horse-mill situated here. Later named after a local school of logicians.

MAGPIE LANE

Gropecuntelane ca. 1230; Croppelane 1238; Gropechunte lane 1249; Grapelone ca. 1251; Gropecountelane 1267; Crope Lane 1483; Group Lane 1814; Winkin Lane 15th c. Dates from a 17th c. alehouse which had the sign of the magpie. Earlier spellings conjure somewhat lurid activities in this passage, no doubt the haunt of knaves, rogues, vagabonds and harlots. 'Winkin' suggests that the London printer Wynkyn de Worde once had a printing press here.

MERTON STREET

Vicus Sancti Johannis 12th c.; Coach and Horses Lane 18th c. (eastern end); *King Street 18th c.* (western end). From St John Baptist Church. Walter de Merton 13th c. lent his name to the nearby college.

NEW INN HALL STREET

North Bayly 1399; Seven Deadly Sins Lane 17th c. SDSL maybe named after 7 poor cottages which stood here. New Inn Hall is part of St Peter's College.

ORIEL STREET

Shidyerdestret ca. 1220; Shideyerde street ca. 1275; St Mary Hall Lane 1772; Oriel Street 19th c. Early spellings probably refer to a palisade. Later form derives from La Oriole (French for *oratoliorum*) the name of a house of Edward III given to the college.

PEMBROKE STREET

Pyneferthynstrete 1363. Originally named after William Penyverthing, Provost of Oxfordshire ca. 1240. Later named from the college.

ST ALDATES

Gret Iury Layne ca. 1215; Fysshestrete 1369; South-Gate Street 1661; Fish Street 1772; St Aldates 19th c. Possibly Oxford's oldest street. Earliest spelling indicates that this was an area occupied by Jews. Later name from the church (maybe a corruption of 'old gate').

TITUP HALL DRIVE

Titup Hall 1797. Maybe from OE *tittup* 'to move in a lively fashion' and applied to horses pulling the Oxford to London coach up nearby Shotover Hill.

TURL STREET

The Turle ca. 1590; Turl Gate Street 1661. Probably refers to a revolving or twirling gate which was in the City Wall at the Broad Street end.

FURTHER READING

Bloxham, C. *Portrait of Oxfordshire.* Hale 1982

Cameron, K. *English Place Names.* Batsford 1996

Ekwall, E. *The Concise Oxford Dictionary of English Place-Names.* Oxford 4th ed. 1960

Gelling, M. *The Place-Names of Oxfordshire.* EPNS Cambridge 1953/54

Gelling, M. *The Place-Names of Berkshire.* EPNS Cambridge 1973/76

Gelling, M. *Place-Names in the Landscape.* Dent 1984

Gelling, M. *The Landscape of Place-Names.* Tyas 2000

Hibbert, C. *The Encyclopædia of Oxford.* Macmillan 1988

Marriott, P. J. *Oxford Street Names Explained.* Marriott 1977

Mills, A. D. *Dictionary of British Place-Names.* Oxford 2003

Smith, A. H. *English Place-Name Elements.* EPNS Cambridge 1956

Whittaker, D. *Cotswold Place-Names: a Concise Dictionary.* Wavestone Press 2005

Magdalen Bridge and the Cherwell, Oxford